Circular Letter Concerning the Preparation and Celebration of the Easter Feasts

JANUARY 16, 1988–VATICAN CITY

Congregation
for Divine Worship

BV
90
.C5
1988

Office of Publishing and Promotion Services
United States Catholic Conference
Washington, D.C.
ISBN 1-55586-219-5

Contents

Preface

1. The Easter Solemnity, revised and restored by Pius XII in 1951, and then the Order of Holy Week in 1955 were favorably received by the Church of the Roman Rite.[1]

The Second Vatican Council, especially in the *Constitution on the Sacred Liturgy*, repeatedly drawing upon tradition, called attention to Christ's paschal mystery and pointed out that it is the font from which all sacraments and sacramentals draw their power.[2]

2. Just as the week has its beginning and climax in the celebration of Sunday, which always has a paschal character, so the summit of the whole liturgical year is in the sacred Easter Triduum of the passion and resurrection of the Lord,[3] which is prepared for by the period of Lent and prolonged for fifty days.

3. In many parts of the Christian world, the faithful followers of Christ, with their pastors, attach great importance to the celebration of this rite and participate in it with great spiritual gain.

However, in some areas where initially the reform of the Easter Vigil was received enthusiastically, it would appear that with the passage of time this enthusiasm has begun to wain. The very concept of the Vigil has almost come to be forgotten in some places, with the result that it is celebrated as if it were an evening Mass, in the same way and at the same time as the Mass celebrated on Saturday evening in anticipation of the Sunday.

It also happens that the celebrations of the Triduum are not held at the correct times. This is because certain devotions and pious exercises are held at more convenient times and so the faithful participate in them rather than in the liturgical celebrations.

Without any doubt, one of the principal reasons for this state of affairs is the inadequate formation given to the clergy and the faithful regarding the paschal mystery as the center of the liturgical year and of Christian life.[4]

---

[1]Cf. Sacred Congregation of Rites (= SCR), Decree *Dominicae Resurrectionis* (February 9, 1951) *Acta Apostolicae Sedis* (= AAS) 43 (1951): 128–137; SCR, Decree *Maxima redemptionis nostrae mysteria* (November 16, 1955) AAS 47 (1955): 838–847.

[2]Cf. Second Vatican Council (= SVC), *Constitution on the Sacred Liturgy (Sacrosanctum Concilium* = SC), nn. 5, 6, 61.

[3]Cf. *General Norms for the Liturgical Year and the Calendar* (= GNLYC), n. 18.

[4]Cf. SVC, *Decree on the Bishops' Pastoral Office in the Church (Christus Dominus)*, n. 15.

4. The holiday period which, in many places today, coincides with Holy Week and certain attitudes held by present day society concur to present difficulties for the faithful to participate in these celebrations.

5. With these points in mind, the Congregation for Divine Worship, after due consideration, thinks that it is a fitting moment to recall certain elements, doctrinal and pastoral, and various norms that have already been published concerning Holy Week. All those details that are given in the liturgical books concerning Lent, Holy Week, the Easter Triduum, and Paschal time retain their full force, unless otherwise stated in this document.

It is the aim of this document that the great mystery of our redemption be celebrated in the best possible way, so that the faithful may participate in it with ever greater spiritual advantage.[5]

---

[5]Cf. *Maxima redemptionis nostrae mysteria*, AAS 47 (1955): 838–847.

I. Lenten Season

6. "The annual lenten season is the fitting time to climb the Holy mountain of Easter.

"The lenten season has a double character, namely, to prepare both catechumens and faithful to celebrate the paschal mystery. The catechumens both with the rite of election and scrutinies, and by catechesis, are prepared for the celebration of the sacraments of Christian initiation; the faithful ever more attentive to the word of God and prayer, prepare themselves by penance for the renewal of their baptismal promises."[6]

A. Concerning the Rite of Christian Initiation

7. The whole rite of Christian initiation has a markedly paschal character, since it is therein that the sacramental participation in the death and resurrection of Christ takes place for the first time. Therefore, Lent should have its full character as a time of purification and enlightenment, especially through the scrutinies and by the presentations; naturally the paschal Vigil should be regarded as the proper time to celebrate the sacraments of initiation.[7]

8. Communities that do not have any catechumens should not, however, fail to pray for those who in the forthcoming paschal Vigil will receive the sacraments of Christian initiation. Pastors should draw the attention of the faithful to those moments of significant importance in their spiritual life, which are nourished by their baptismal profession of faith, and which they will be invited to renew in the Easter Vigil—"the fullness of the lenten observance."[8]

9. In Lent, there should be catechesis for those adults who, although baptized when infants, were not brought up in the faith and, consequently, have not been confirmed nor have they received the Eucharist. During this period, penitential services should be arranged to help prepare them for the sacrament of reconciliation.[9]

---

[6]*Caeremoniale episcoporum* (= CE), n. 249.

[7]Cf. *The Roman Ritual*, "Rite of Christian Initiation of Adults" (= RCIA), n. 8; *Code of Canon Law* (= CIC), c. 856.

[8]*Roman Missal*, "The Easter Vigil," n. 46.

[9]Cf. RCIA, IV, esp. n. 303.

10. The lenten season is also an appropriate time for the celebration of penitential rites on the model of the scrutinies for unbaptized children who are at an age to be catechized and also for children already baptized, before being admitted to the sacrament of penance.[10]

The bishop should have particular care to foster the catechumenate of both adults and children and, according to circumstances, to preside at the prescribed rites, with the devout participation of the local community.[11]

B. Celebrations during the Lenten Season

11. The Sundays of Lent take precedence over all feasts and all solemnities. Solemnities occurring on these Sundays are observed on the preceding Saturday.[12] The weekdays of Lent have precedence over obligatory memorials.[13]

12. The catechesis on the paschal mystery and the sacraments should be given a special place in the Sunday homilies. The text of the *Lectionary* should be carefully explained, particularly the passages of the Gospel that illustrate the diverse aspects of baptism and the other sacraments and the mercy of God.

13. Pastors should frequently and as fully as possible explain the word of God in homilies on weekdays, in celebrations of the word of God, in penitential celebrations,[14] in various reunions, in visiting families, or on the occasion of blessing families. The faithful should try and attend weekday Mass and where this is not possible they should at least be encouraged to read the lessons, either with their family or in private.

14. "The lenten season should retain something of its penitential character."[15] "As regards catechesis, it is important to impress on the minds of the faithful not only the social consequences of sin but also that aspect of the virtue of penance, which involves the detestation of sin as an offense against God."[16]

The virtue and practice of penance form a necessary part of the preparation for Easter. From that inner conversion of heart should spring the practice of penance, both for the individual Christian and the whole community; which, while being adapted to the conditions of the present time,

---

[10]Cf. ibid., nn. 303–333.

[11]Cf. CE, nn. 250, 406–407; RCIA, n. 41.

[12]Cf. GNLYC, n. 5; also see GNLYC, n. 56f, in *Notitiae* 23 (1987): 397.

[13]Ibid., n. 16b.

[14]See *General Instruction of the Roman Missal* (= GIRM), n. 42; "Rite of Penance," nn. 36–37.

[15]Pope Paul VI, Apostolic Constitution *Paenitemini*, II, 1; AAS 58 (1966): 183.

[16]CE, n. 251.

should nevertheless witness to the evangelical spirit of penance and also be to the advantage of others.

The role of the Church in penitential practices is not to be neglected and encouragement is to be given to pray for sinners. This intention should be included in the prayer of the faithful.[17]

15. "The faithful are to be encouraged to participate in an ever more intense and fruitful way in the lenten liturgy and in penitential celebrations. They are to be clearly reminded that both according to the law and tradition, they should approach the sacrament of penance during this season, so that with purified heart they may participate in the paschal mysteries. It is appropriate that during Lent the sacrament of penance be celebrated according to the rite for the reconciliation of several penitents with individual confession and absolution, as given in the *Roman Ritual.*"[18]

Pastors should devote themselves to the ministry of reconciliation and provide sufficient time for the faithful to avail themselves of this sacrament.

16. "All lenten observances should be of such a nature that they also witness to the life of the local Church and foster it. The Roman tradition of the 'stational' churches can be recommended as a model for gathering the faithful in one place. In this way, the faithful can assemble in larger numbers, especially under the leadership of the bishop of the diocese, or at the tombs of the saints, or in the principle churches of the city or sanctuaries, or some place of pilgrimage which has a special significance for the diocese."[19]

17. "In Lent, the altar should not be decorated with flowers, and musical instruments may be played only to give necessary support to the singing."[20] This is in order that the penitential character of the season be preserved.

18. Likewise, from the beginning of Lent until to the paschal Vigil, "Alleluia" is to be omitted in all celebrations, even on solemnities and feasts.[21]

19. The chants to be sung in celebrations, especially of the Eucharist, and also at devotional exercises should be in harmony with the spirit of the season and the liturgical texts.

20. Devotional exercises that harmonize with the lenten season are to be encouraged, for example, "The Stations of the Cross." They should help foster the liturgical spirit with which the faithful can prepare themselves for the celebration of Christ's paschal mystery.

---

[17]Cf. ibid.; SC, n. 109.

[18]CE, n. 251.

[19]CE, n. 260.

[20]CE, n. 252.

[21]Cf. GNLYC, n. 28.

C. Particular Details Concerning the Days of Lent

21. "On the Wednesday before the first Sunday of Lent, the faithful receive the ashes, thus entering into the time established for the purification of their souls. This sign of penance, a traditionally biblical one, has been preserved among the Church's customs until the present day. It signifies the human condition of the sinner, who seeks to express his guilt before the Lord in an exterior manner, and by so doing express his interior conversion, led on by the confident hope that the Lord will be merciful. This same sign marks the beginning of the way of conversion, which is developed through the celebration of the sacraments of penance during the days before Easter."[22]

The blessing and imposition of ashes should take place either in the Mass or outside of the Mass. In the latter case, it is to be part of a liturgy of the word and conclude with the prayer of the faithful.[23]

22. Ash Wednesday is to be observed as a day of penance in the whole Church, one of both abstinence and fasting.[24]

23. The first Sunday of Lent marks the beginning of the annual lenten observance.[25] In the Mass of this Sunday, there should be some distinctive elements that underline this important moment (e.g., the entrance procession with litanies of the saints).[26] During the Mass of the first Sunday in Lent, the bishop should celebrate the rite of election in the cathedral or in some other church, as seems appropriate.[27]

24. The gospel pericopes of the Samaritan woman, of the man blind from birth, and the resurrection of Lazarus are assigned to the III, IV, and V Sundays of Lent of year A. Of particular significance in relation to Christian initiation, they can also be read in years B and C, especially in places where there are catechumens.[28]

25. On the fourth Sunday of Lent, *Laetare,* and in solemnities and feasts, musical instruments may be played and the altar decorated with flowers. Rose colored vestments may be worn on this Sunday.[29]

26. The practice of covering the crosses and images in the church may be observed, if the episcopal conference should so decide. The crosses are to be covered until the end of the celebration of the Lord's passion on Good Friday. Images are to remain covered until the beginning of the Easter Vigil.[30]

---

[22]CE, n. 253.

[23]Cf. *Roman Missal,* "Ash Wednesday."

[24]Cf. *Paenitemini,* II, 1; AAS 58 (1966): 183.

[25]Cf. *Roman Missal,* "First Sunday of Lent," Opening Prayer and Prayer over the Gifts.

[26]Cf. CE, n. 261.

[27]Cf. CE, nn. 408–410.

[28]Cf. *Roman Missal,* "Lectionary for Mass," Second Edition (1981), Introduction, n. 97.

[29]Cf. CE, n. 252.

[30]Cf. *Roman Missal,* rubric "Saturday of the Fourth Week of Lent."

II. Holy Week

27. During Holy Week, the Church celebrates the mysteries of salvation accomplished by Christ in the last days of his life on earth, beginning with his messianic entrance into Jerusalem.

The lenten season lasts until the Thursday of this week. The Easter Triduum begins with the evening Mass of the Lord's Supper, is continued through Good Friday with the celebration of the passion of the Lord and Holy Saturday, to reach its summit in the Easter Vigil, and concludes with Vespers of Easter Sunday.

"The days of Holy Week, from Monday to Thursday inclusive, have precedence over all other celebrations."[31] It is not fitting that baptisms and confirmation be celebrated on these days.

A. Passion Sunday (Palm Sunday)

28. Holy Week begins on Passion (or Palm) Sunday, which joins the foretelling of Christ's regal triumph and the proclamation of the passion. The connection between both aspects of the paschal mystery should be shown and explained in the celebration and catechesis of this day.[32]

29. The commemoration of the entrance of the Lord into Jerusalem has, according to ancient custom, been celebrated with a solemn procession, in which the faithful in song and gesture imitate the Hebrew children who went to meet the Lord, singing "Hosanna."[33]

The procession may take place only once, before the Mass that has the largest attendance, even if this should be in the evening of either Saturday or Sunday. The congregation should assemble in a secondary church or chapel or in some other suitable place distinct from the church to which the procession will move.

In this procession, the faithful carry palm or other branches. The priest and the ministers, also carrying branches, precede the people.[34]

---

[31]GNLYC, n. 16a.

[32]Cf. CE, n. 263.

[33]Cf. *Roman Missal*, "Passion Sunday (Palm Sunday)," n. 16.

[34]Cf. CE, n. 270.

The palms or branches are blessed so that they can be carried in the procession. The palms should be taken home, where they will serve as a reminder of the victory of Christ, which they celebrated in the procession.

Pastors should make every effort to ensure that this procession in honor of Christ the King be so prepared and celebrated that it is of great spiritual significance in the life of the faithful.

30. The *Missal*, in order to commemorate the entrance of the Lord into Jerusalem, in addition to the solemn procession described above, gives two other forms, not simply for convenience, but to provide for those situations when it will not be possible to have the procession.

The second form is that of a solemn entrance, when the procession cannot take place outside of the church. The third form is a simple entrance such as is used at all Masses on this Sunday that do not have the solemn entrance.[35]

31. Where the Mass cannot be celebrated, there should be a celebration of the word of God on the theme of the Lord's messianic entrance and passion, either on Saturday evening or on Sunday at a convenient time.[36]

32. During the procession, the choir and people should sing the chants proposed in the *Roman Missal*, especially Psalms 23 and 46, as well as other appropriate songs in honor of Christ the King.

33. The passion narrative occupies a special place. It should be sung or read in the traditional way, that is, by three persons who take the part of Christ, the narrator, and the people. The passion is proclaimed by deacons or priests, or by lay readers. In the latter case, the part of the Christ should be reserved to the priest.

The proclamation of the passion should be without candles and incense; the greeting and the signs of the cross are omitted; and only a deacon asks for the blessing, as he does before the Gospel.[37]

For the spiritual good of the faithful, the passion should be proclaimed in its entirety, and the readings that proceed it should not be omitted.

34. After the passion has been proclaimed, a homily is to be given.

---

[35]Cf. *Roman Missal*, "Passion Sunday," n. 16.

[36]Cf. ibid., n. 19.

[37]Cf. ibid., n. 22. For a Mass at which a bishop presides, cf. CE, n. 74.

B. The Chrism Mass

35. The Chrism Mass, which the bishop concelebrates with his presbyterium, and at which the Holy Chrism is consecrated and the oils blessed, manifests the communion of the priests with their bishop in the same priesthood and ministry of Christ.[38] The priests who concelebrate with the bishop should come to this Mass from different parts of the diocese, thus showing in the consecration of the Chrism to be his witnesses and cooperators, just as in their daily ministry, they are his helpers and counselors.

The faithful are also to be encouraged to participate in this Mass and to receive the sacrament of the Eucharist.

Traditionally, the Chrism Mass is celebrated on the Thursday of Holy Week. If, however, it should prove to be difficult for the clergy and people to gather with the bishop, this rite can be transferred to another day, but one always close to Easter.[39] The Chrism and the oil of catechumens is to be used in the celebration of the sacraments of initiation on Easter night.

36. There should be only one celebration of the Chrism Mass, given its significance in the life of the diocese, and it should take place in the cathedral or, for pastoral reasons, in another church[40] that has a special significance.

The Holy oils can be brought to the individual parishes before the celebration of the evening Mass of the Lord's Supper, or at some other suitable time. This can be a means of catechizing the faithful about the use and effects of the Holy oils and Chrism in Christian life.

C. The Penitential Celebrations in Lent

37. It is fitting that the lenten season should be concluded, both for the individual Christian as well as for the whole Christian community, with a penitential celebration, so that they may be helped to prepare to celebrate more fully the paschal mystery.[41]

These celebrations, however, should take place before the Easter Triduum and should not immediately precede the evening Mass of the Lord's Supper.

---

[38]Cf. SVC, *Decree on the Ministry and Life of Priests (Presbyterorum Ordinis)*, n. 7.

[39]Cf. CE, n. 275.

[40]Cf. CE, n. 276.

[41]Cf. *Rite of Penance*, "Appendix II," nn. 1, 7. Cf. *supra* n. 18.

III. The Easter Triduum in General

38. The greatest mysteries of the redemption are celebrated yearly by the Church, beginning with the evening Mass of the Lord's Supper on Holy Thursday and ending with Vespers of Easter Sunday. This time is called "the triduum of the crucified, buried and risen"; [42] it is also called the "Easter Triduum" because during it is celebrated the paschal mystery, that is, the passing of the Lord from this world to his Father. The Church, by the celebration of this mystery through liturgical signs and sacramentals, is united to Christ, her Spouse, in intimate communion.

39. The Easter fast is sacred on the first two days of the Triduum, in which, according to ancient tradition, the Church fasts "because the Spouse has been taken away."[43] Good Friday is a day of fasting and abstinence; it is also recommended that Holy Saturday be so observed, so that the Church, with uplifted and welcoming heart, be ready to celebrate the joys of the Sunday of the Resurrection.[44]

40. It is recommended that there be a communal celebration of the Office of Readings and Morning Prayer on Good Friday and Holy Saturday. It is fitting that the bishop should celebrate the Office in the cathedral with, as far as possible, the participation of the clergy and people.[45]

This Office, formerly called *Tenebrae*, held a special place in the devotion of the faithful as they meditated upon the passion, death, and burial of the Lord while awaiting the announcement of the resurrection.

41. For the celebration of the Easter Triduum, it is necessary that there be a sufficient number of ministers and assistants who should be prepared so that they know what their role is in the celebration. Pastors must ensure that the meaning of each part of the celebration be explained to the faithful so that they may participate more fully and fruitfully.

42. The chants of the people, and also of the ministers and the celebrating priest, are of special importance in the celebration of Holy Week and par-

---

[42]Cf. *Maxima redemptionis nostrae mysteria*, AAS 47 (1955): 858. St. AUGUSTINE, Ep. 55, 24, PL, 35: 215.

[43]Mk 2:19–20; TERTULLIAN, *De ieiunio* 2 et 13, Corpus Christianorum II, p. 1271.

[44]Cf. CE, n. 295; SC, n. 110.

[45]Cf. CE, n. 296.

ticularly of the Easter Triduum because they add to the solemnity of these days and also because the texts are more effective when sung.

The episcopal conferences are asked, unless provision has already been made, to provide music for those parts which should always be sung, namely:

a) the general intercessions of Good Friday; the deacon's invitation and the acclamation of the people;

b) chants for the showing and veneration of the cross;

c) the acclamations during the procession with the paschal candle and the Easter proclamation, the responsorial "Alleluia," the litany of the saints, and the acclamation after the blessing of water.

Since the purpose of sung texts is also to facilitate the participation of the faithful, they should not be lightly omitted; such texts should be set to music. If the text for use in the liturgy has not yet been set to music, it is possible, as a temporary measure, to select other similar texts that are set to music. It is, however, fitting that there should be a collection of texts set to music for these celebrations, paying special attention to:

a) chants for the procession and blessing of palms, and for the entrance into church;

b) chants to accompany the procession with the Holy oils;

c) chants to accompany the procession with the gifts on Holy Thursday in the evening Mass of the Lord's Supper, and hymns to accompany the procession of the Blessed Sacrament to the place of repose;

d) the responsorial psalms at the Easter Vigil, and chants to accompany the sprinkling with blessed water.

Music should be provided for the passion narrative, the Easter proclamation, and the blessing of baptismal water. Obviously, the melodies should be of a simple nature in order to facilitate their use.

In larger churches where the resources permit, a more ample use should be made of the Church's musical heritage, both ancient and modern, always ensuring that this does not impede the active participation of the faithful.

43. It is fitting that small religious communities, both clerical and lay, and other lay groups should participate in the celebration of the Easter Triduum in neighboring principal churches.[46]

Similarly, where the number of participants and ministers is so small that the celebrations of the Easter Triduum cannot be carried out with the

---

[46]Cf. SCR, Instruction *Eucharisticum mysterium* (= EM) (May 25, 1967), n. 26. AAS 59 (1967): 558. N.B.: In monasteries of nuns, every effort should be made to celebrate the Easter Triduum with the greatest possible ceremony, but within the monastery church.

requisite solemnity, such groups of the faithful should assemble in a larger church.

Also, where there are small parishes with only one priest, it is recommended that such parishes should assemble, as far as possible, in a principal church and participate in the celebrations there.

On account of the needs of the faithful, where a pastor has the responsibility for two or more parishes in which the faithful assemble in large numbers, and where the celebrations can be carried out with the requisite care and solemnity, the celebrations of the Easter Triduum may be repeated in accord with the given norms.[47]

So that seminary students "might live fully Christ's paschal mystery, and thus be able to teach those who will be committed to their care,"[48] they should be given a thorough and comprehensive liturgical formation. It is important that during their formative years in the seminary, they should experience fruitfully the solemn Easter celebrations, especially those over which the bishop presides.[49]

---

[47]Cf. SCR, *Ordinationes et declarationes circa Ordinem hebdomadae sanctae instauratum* (February 1, 1957), n. 21; AAS 49 (1957): 91–95.

[48]SVC, *Decree on Priestly Formation (Optatam Totius)*, n. 8.

[49]Cf. Congregation for Catholic Education, *Instruction on Liturgical Formation in Seminaries* (May 17, 1979), nn. 15, 33.

IV. Holy Thursday Evening Mass of the Lord's Supper

44. With the celebration of Mass on the evening of Holy Thursday, "the Church begins the Easter Triduum and recalls the Last Supper in which the Lord Jesus, on the night he was betrayed, showing his love for those who were his own in the world, he gave his body and blood under the species of bread and wine offering to his Father and giving them to the Apostles so that they might partake of them, and he commanded them and their successors in the priesthood to perpetuate this offering."[50]

45. Careful attention should be given to the mysteries that are commemorated in this Mass: the institution of the Eucharist, the institution of the priesthood, and Christ's command of brotherly love; the homily should explain these points.

46. The Mass of the Lord's Supper is celebrated in the evening, at a time that is more convenient for the full participation of the whole local community. All priests may concelebrate, even if on this day they have already concelebrated the Chrism Mass or if, for the good of the faithful, they must celebrate another Mass.[51]

47. Where pastoral considerations require it, the local ordinary may permit another Mass to be celebrated in churches and oratories in the evening and, in the case of true necessity, even in the morning, but only for those faithful who cannot otherwise participate in the evening Mass. Care should nevertheless be taken to ensure that celebrations of this kind do not take place for the benefit of private persons or of small groups, and that they are not to the detriment of the main Mass.

According to the ancient tradition of the Church, all Masses without the participation of the people are forbidden on this day.[52]

48. The tabernacle should be completely empty before the celebration.[53] Hosts for the communion of the faithful should be consecrated during that

---

[50]CE, n. 297.
[51]Cf. *Roman Missal*, "Evening Mass of the Lord's Supper."
[52]Cf. ibid.
[53]Cf. ibid., n. 1.

celebration.[54] A sufficient amount of bread should be consecrated to provide also for communion on the following day.

49. For the reservation of Blessed Sacrament, a place should be prepared and adorned in such a way as to be conducive to prayer and meditation; that sobriety appropriate to the liturgy of these days is enjoined, to the avoidance or suppression of all abuses.[55]

When the tabernacle is in a chapel separated from the central part of the church, it is appropriate to prepare the place of repose and adoration there.

50. During the singing of the hymn *"Gloria in excelsis,"* in accordance with local custom, the bells may be rung but should thereafter remain silent until the *"Gloria in excelsis"* of the Easter Vigil, unless the conference of bishops or the local ordinary, for a suitable reason, has decided otherwise.[56] During this same period, the organ and other musical instruments may be used only for the purpose of supporting the singing.[57]

51. The washing of the feet of chosen men which, according to tradition, is performed on this day, represents the service and charity of Christ, who came "not to be served, but to serve."[58] This tradition should be maintained, and its proper significance explained.

52. Gifts for the poor, especially those collected during Lent as the fruit of penance, may be presented in the offertory procession while the people sing *"Ubi caritas est vera."*[59]

53. It is more appropriate that the Eucharist be borne directly from the altar by the deacons or acolytes, or extraordinary ministers, at the moment of communion for the sick and infirm who must communicate at home, so that, in this way, they may be more closely united to the celebrating Church.

54. After the postcommunion prayer, the procession forms with the crossbearer at its head. The Blessed Sacrament, accompanied by lighted candles and incense, is carried through the church to the place of reservation, to the singing of the hymn *"Pange lingua"* or some other eucharistic song.[60] This rite of transfer of the Blessed Sacrament may not be carried out

---

[54]SC, n. 55; EM, n. 31. AAS 59 (1967): 557–558.

[55]Cf. *Maxima redemptionis nostrae mysteria*, n. 9, AAS 47 (1955): 895.

[56]Cf. *Roman Missal*, "Evening Mass of the Lord's Supper."

[57]CF. CE, n. 300.

[58]Mt 20:28.

[59]Cf. CE, n. 303.

[60]Cf. *Roman Missal*, "Evening Mass of the Lord's Supper," nn. 15–16.

if the liturgy of the Lord's passion will not be celebrated in that same church on the following day.[61]

55. The Blessed Sacrament should be reserved in a closed tabernacle or pyx. Under no circumstances may it be exposed in a monstrance.

The place where the tabernacle or pyx is situated must not be made to resemble a tomb, and the expression *tomb* is to be avoided: for the chapel of repose is not prepared so as to represent the "Lord's burial" but for the custody of the eucharistic bread that will be distributed in communion on Good Friday.

56. After the Mass of the Lord's Supper, the faithful should be encouraged to spend a suitable period of time during the night in the church in adoration before the Blessed Sacrament that has been solemnly reserved. Where appropriate, this prolonged eucharistic adoration may be accompanied by the reading of some part of the gospel of Saint John (ch. 13–17).

From midnight onward, however, the adoration should be made without external solemnity, for the day of the Lord's passion has begun.[62]

57. After Mass, the altar should be stripped. It is fitting that any crosses in the church be covered with a red or purple veil, unless they have already been veiled on the Saturday before the fifth Sunday of Lent. Lamps should not be lit before the images of saints.

[61]Cf. SCR, "Declaration of March 15, 1956," n. 3, AAS 48 (1956): 153; *Ordinationes et declarationes circa Ordinem hebdomadae sanctae instauratum*, n. 15, AAS 49 (1957): 93.

[62]Cf. *Roman Missal*, "Evening Mass of the Lord's Supper," n. 21; *Maxima redemptionis nostrae mysteria*, nn. 8–10, AAS 47 (1955): 845.

V. Good Friday

58. On this day, when "Christ our passover was sacrificed,"[63] the Church meditates on the passion of her Lord and Spouse, adores the cross, commemorates her origin from the side of Christ asleep on the cross, and intercedes for the salvation of the whole world.

59. On this day, in accordance with ancient tradition, the Church does not celebrate the Eucharist: Holy Communion is distributed to the faithful during the celebration of the Lord's passion alone, though it may be brought at any time of the day to the sick who cannot take part in the celebration.[64]

60. Good Friday is a day of penance to be observed as an obligation in the whole Church, and indeed, through abstinence and fasting.[65]

61. All celebration of the sacraments on this day is strictly prohibited, except for the sacraments of penance and anointing of the sick.[66] Funerals are to be celebrated without singing, music, or the tolling of bells.

62. It is recommended that on this day the Office of Readings and Morning Prayer, be celebrated with the participation of the people in the churches (cf. n. 40).

63. The celebration of the Lord's passion is to take place in the afternoon, at about three o'clock. For pastoral reasons, an appropriate time will be chosen in order to allow the people to assemble more easily, for example, shortly after midday or in the late evening, however not later than nine o'clock.[67]

64. The order for the celebration of the Lord's passion (the liturgy of the word, the adoration of the cross, and Holy Communion) that stems from an ancient tradition of the Church should be observed faithfully and religiously and may not be changed by anyone on his own initiative.

65. The priest and ministers proceed to the altar in silence, without any singing. If any words of introduction are to be said, they should be pronounced before the ministers enter.

---

[63]1 Cor 5:7.

[64]Cf. *Roman Missal,* "Good Friday," Celebration of the Lord's Passion, nn. 1, 3.

[65]*Paenitemini,* II, 2; AAS 58 (1966): 183, CIC, c. 1251.

[66]Cf. *Roman Missal,* "Good Friday," Celebration of the Lord's Passion, n. 1. *Ad Missale Romanum,* in *Notitiae* 13 (1977); 602.

[67]Cf. ibid., n. 3. *Ordinationes et declarationes circa Ordinem hebdomadae sanctae instauratum,* n. 15, AAS 49 (1957): 94.

The priest and ministers make a reverence to the altar, prostrating themselves. This act of prostration, which is proper to the rite of the day, should be strictly observed for it signifies both the abasement of "earthly man,"[68] and also the grief and sorrow of the Church.

As the ministers enter, the faithful should be standing, and thereafter should kneel in silent prayer.

66. The readings are to be read in their entirety. The responsorial psalm and the chant before the gospel are to be sung in the usual manner. The narrative of the Lord's passion according to John is sung or read in the way prescribed for the previous Sunday (cf. n. 33). After the reading of the passion, a homily should be given, at the end of which the faithful may be invited to spend a short time in meditation.[69]

67. The general intercessions are to follow the wording and form handed down by ancient tradition, maintaining the full range of intentions, so as to signify clearly the universal effect of the passion of Christ, who hung on the cross for the salvation of the whole world. In case of grave public necessity, the local ordinary may permit or prescribe the adding of special intentions.[70]

In this event, it is permitted to the priest to select from the prayers of the *Missal* those intercessions more appropriate to local circumstances, in such a way, however, that the series follows the rule for general intercessions.[71]

68. For veneration of the cross, let a cross be used that is of appropriate size and beauty, and let one or other of the forms for this rite as found in the *Roman Missal* be followed. The rite should be carried out with the splendor worthy of the mystery of our salvation. Both the invitation pronounced at the unveiling of the cross and the people's response should be made in song, and a period of respectful silence is to be observed after each act of veneration, with the celebrant standing and holding the raised cross.

69. The cross is to be presented to each of the faithful individually for their adoration, since the personal adoration of the cross is a most important feature in this celebration. Only when necessitated by the large numbers of faithful present should the rite of veneration be made simultaneously by all present.[72]

---

[68]Cf. ibid., n. 5; alternative prayer.

[69]Cf. ibid., n. 9; CE, n. 319.

[70]Cf. ibid., n. 12.

[71]Cf. GIRM, n. 46.

[72]Cf. *Roman Missal*, "Good Friday," Celebration of the Lord's Passion, n. 19.

Only one cross should be used for the veneration, as this contributes to the full symbolism of the rite. During the veneration of the cross, the antiphons, "Reproaches," and hymns should be sung so that the history of salvation be commemorated through song.[73] Other appropriate songs may also be sung (cf n. 42).

70. The priest sings the invitation to the Lord's Prayer, which is then sung by all. The sign of peace is not exchanged. The communion rite is as described in the *Missal*.

During the distribution of communion, Psalm 21 or another suitable song may be sung. When communion has been distributed, the pyx is taken to a place prepared for it outside of the church.

71. After the celebration, the altar is stripped; the cross remains, however, with four candles. An appropriate place (for example, the chapel of repose used for reservation of the Eucharist on Maundy Thursday) can be prepared within the church, and there the Lord's cross is placed so that the faithful may venerate and kiss it and spend some time in meditation.

72. Devotions, such as the Way of the Cross, processions of the passion, and commemorations of the sorrows of the Blessed Virgin Mary are not, for pastoral reasons, to be neglected. The texts and songs used, however, should be adapted to the spirit of the liturgy of this day. Such devotions should be assigned to a time of day that makes it quite clear that the liturgical celebration, by its very nature, far surpasses them in importance.[74]

---

[73]Cf. Mi 6:3–4.
[74]Cf. SC, n. 13.

VI. Holy Saturday

73. On Holy Saturday, the Church is, as it were, at the Lord's tomb, meditating on his passion and death and on his descent into hell,[75] awaiting his resurrection with prayer and fasting. It is highly recommended that on this day, the Office of Readings and Morning Prayer be celebrated with the participation of the people (cf. n. 40).[76] Where this cannot be done, there should be some celebration of the word of God or some act of devotion suited to the mystery celebrated this day.

74. The image of Christ crucified or lying in the tomb or the descent into hell, which mystery Holy Saturday recalls, as also an image of the sorrowful Virgin Mary, can be placed in the church for the veneration of the faithful.

75. On this day, the Church abstains strictly from celebration of the sacrifice of the Mass.[77] Holy Communion may only be given in the form of Viaticum. The celebration of marriages is forbidden, as is also the celebration of other sacraments, except those of penance and the anointing of the sick.

76. The faithful are to be instructed on the special character of Holy Saturday.[78] Festive customs and traditions associated with this day because of the former practice of anticipating the celebration of Easter on Holy Saturday should be reserved for Easter night and the day that follows.

---

[75]Cf. *Roman Missal*, "Holy Saturday"; Apostles' Creed; 1 Pt 3:19.

[76]Cf. *General Instruction of the Liturgy of the Hours* (= GILOTH), n. 210.

[77]Cf. *Roman Missal*, "Holy Saturday."

[78]*Maxima redemptionis nostrae mysteria*, AAS 47 (1955): 843.

VII. Easter Sunday of the Lord's Resurrection

A. The Easter Vigil

77. According to a most ancient tradition, this night is "one of vigil for the Lord,"[79] and the Vigil celebrated during it, to commemorate that holy night when the Lord rose from the dead, is regarded as the "mother of all holy vigils."[80] For in that night, the Church keeps vigil, waiting for the resurrection of the Lord, and celebrates the sacraments of Christian initiation.[81]

1. The Meaning of the Nocturnal Character of the Easter Vigil

78. "The entire celebration of the Easter Vigil takes place at night. It should not begin before nightfall; it should end before daybreak on Sunday."[82] This rule is to be taken according to its strictest sense. Reprehensible are those abuses and practices that have crept into many places in violation of this ruling, whereby the Easter Vigil is celebrated at the time of day that it is customary to celebrate anticipated Sunday Masses.[83]

Those reasons that have been advanced in some quarters for the anticipation of the Easter Vigil, such as lack of public order, are not put forward in connection with Christmas night nor other gatherings of various kinds.

79. The Passover Vigil, in which the Hebrews kept watch for the Lord's passover which was to free them from slavery to Pharaoh, is an annual commemoration. It prefigured the true Pasch of Christ that was to come, the night that is of true liberation, in which "destroying the bonds of death, Christ rose as victor from the depths."[84]

---

[79]Ex 12:42.

[80]St. AUGUSTINE, *Sermo* 219, PL 38: 1088.

[81]Cf. CE, n. 332.

[82]Ibid.; Cf. *Roman Missal*, "The Easter Vigil," n. 3.

[83]Cf. EM, n. 28. AAS 59 (1967): 556–557.

[84]*Roman Missal*, "The Easter Vigil," n. 19, Easter Proclamation.

80. From the very outset, the Church has celebrated that annual Pasch, which is the solemnity of solemnities, above all by means of a night vigil. For the resurrection of Christ is the foundation of our faith and hope, and through baptism and confirmation, we are inserted into the paschal mystery of Christ, dying, buried, and raised with him, and with him, we shall also reign.[85]

The full meaning of Vigil is a waiting for the coming of the Lord.[86]

2. The Structure of the Easter Vigil and the Significance of Its Different Elements and Parts

81. The order for the Easter Vigil is arranged so that after the service of light and the Easter proclamation (which is the first part of the Vigil), Holy Church meditates on the wonderful works that the Lord God wrought for his people from the earliest times (the second part or liturgy of the word) to the moment when, together with those new members reborn in baptism (third part), she is called to the table prepared by the Lord for his Church, the commemoration of his death and resurrection, until he comes (fourth part).[87]

This liturgical order must not be changed by anyone on his own initiative.

82. The first part consists of symbolic acts and gestures, which require that they be performed in all their fullness and nobility so that their meaning, as explained by the introductory words of the celebrant and the liturgical prayers, may be truly understood by the faithful.

Insofar as possible, a suitable place should be prepared outside the church for the blessing of the new fire, whose flames should be such that they genuinely dispel the darkness and light up the night.

The paschal candle should be prepared, which for effective symbolism must be made of wax, never be artificial, be renewed each year, be only one in number, and be of sufficiently large size so that it may evoke the truth that Christ is the light of the world. It is blessed with the signs and words prescribed in the *Missal* or by the conference of bishops.[88]

---

[85]SC, n. 6; Cf. Rom 6:3–6; Eph 2:5–6; Col 2:12–13; 2 Tm 2:11–12.

[86]"We keep vigil on that night because the Lord rose from the dead; that life . . . where there is no longer the sleep of death, began for us in his flesh; being thus risen, death will be no more nor have dominion. . . . If we have kept vigil for the risen one, he will see that we shall reign with him for ever." St. AUGUSTINE, *Sermo Guelferbytan,* 5, 4, PLS 2: 552.

[87]Cf. *Roman Missal,* "The Easter Vigil," n. 7.

[88]Cf. ibid., nn. 10–12.

83. The procession, by which the people enter the church, should be led by the light of the paschal candle alone. Just as the children of Israel were guided at night by a pillar of fire, so similarly Christians follow the risen Christ. To each response, "Thanks be to God," there is no reason why there should not be added some acclamation in honor of Christ.

The light from the paschal candle should be gradually passed to the candles that all present are holding in their hands; the electric lighting should be switched off.

84. The deacon makes the Easter proclamation, which tells by means of a great poetic text the whole Easter mystery, placed in the context of the economy of salvation. In case of necessity, where there is no deacon and the celebrating priest is unable to sing it, a cantor may do so. The bishops' conferences may adapt this proclamation by inserting into it acclamations from the people.[89]

85. The readings from Sacred Scripture constitute the second part of the Vigil. They give an account of the outstanding deeds of the history of salvation, which the faithful are helped to meditate calmly upon by the singing of the responsorial psalm, by a silent pause, and by the celebrant's prayer.

The restored order for the Vigil has seven readings from the Old Testament, chosen from the law and the prophets, which are everywhere in use according to the most ancient tradition of East and West; and two readings from the New Testament, namely, from the apostles and from the gospel. Thus, the Church, "beginning with Moses and all the prophets," explains Christ's paschal mystery.[90] Consequently, wherever this is possible, all the readings should be read in order so that the character of the Easter Vigil, which demands that it be somewhat prolonged, be respected at all costs.

Where, however, pastoral conditions require that the number of readings be reduced, there should be at least three readings from the Old Testament, taken from the law and the prophets; and the reading from Exodus (ch. 14), with its canticle, must never be omitted.[91]

86. The typological import of the Old Testament texts is rooted in the New and is made plain by the prayer pronounced by the celebrating priest after each reading; but it will also be helpful to introduce the people to the meaning of each reading by means of a brief introduction. This introduction may be given by the priest himself or by a deacon.

---

[89]Cf. ibid., n. 17.

[90]Lk 24:27, 44–45.

[91]Cf. *Roman Missal*, "The Easter Vigil," n. 21.

National or diocesan liturgical commissions will prepare aids for pastors.
Each reading is followed by the singing of a psalm, to which the people respond.

Melodies that are capable of promoting the people's participation and devotion should be provided for these responses.[92] Great care is to be taken that trivial songs do not take the place of the psalms.

87. After the readings from the Old Testament and the hymn "*Gloria in excelsis,*" the bells are rung in accordance with local custom, the collect is recited, and the celebration moves on to the readings from the New Testament. There is read an exhortation from the apostles on baptism as an insertion into Christ's paschal mystery.

Then all stand and the priest intones the "Alleluia" three times, each time raising the pitch. The people repeat it after him.[93] If it is necessary, the psalmist or cantor may sing the "Alleluia," which the people then take up as an acclamation to be interspersed between the verses of Psalm 117, which is so often cited by the apostles in their Easter preaching.[94] Finally, the resurrection of the Lord is proclaimed from the gospel as the high point of the whole liturgy of the word. After the gospel, a homily is to be given, no matter how brief.

88. The third part of the Vigil is the baptismal liturgy. Christ's passover and ours are celebrated. This is given full expression in those churches that have a baptismal font, and more so when the Christian initiation of adults is held, or at least the baptism of infants.[95] Even if there are no candidates for baptism, the blessing of baptismal water should still take place in parish churches. If this blessing does not take place at the baptismal font but in the sanctuary, baptismal water should be carried afterwards to the baptistery, there to be kept throughout the whole of paschal time.[96] Where there are neither candidates for baptism nor any need to bless the font, baptism should be commemorated by the blessing of water destined for sprinkling upon the people.[97]

89. Next follows the renewal of baptismal promises, introduced by some words on the part of the celebrating priest. The faithful reply to the questions put to them, standing and holding lighted candles in their hands.

---

[92]Cf. ibid., n. 23.

[93]Cf. CE, n. 352.

[94]Cf. Acts 4:11–12; Mt 21:42; Mk 12:10; Lk 20:17.

[95]Cf. *The Roman Ritual,* "Rite of Baptism for Children," n. 6.

[96]Cf. *Roman Missal,* "The Easter Vigil," n. 48.

[97]Cf. ibid., n. 45.

They are then sprinkled with water; in this way the gestures and words recall to them the baptism they have received. The celebrating priest sprinkles the people by passing through the main part of the church while all sing the antiphon *"Vidi aquam"* or another suitable song of a baptismal character.[98]

90. The celebration of the Eucharist forms the fourth part of the Vigil and marks its high point, for it is in the fullest sense the Easter Sacrament, that is to say, the commemoration of the sacrifice of the cross and the presence of the risen Christ, the completion of Christian initiation, and the foretaste of the eternal pasch.

91. Great care should be taken that this eucharistic liturgy is not celebrated in haste, indeed, all the rites and words must be given their full force: the general intercessions, in which the neophytes for the first time as members of the faithful exercise their priesthood; [99] the procession at the offertory, in which the neophytes, if there are any, take part; the first, second, or third Eucharistic Prayer, preferably sung, with the proper embolisms;[100] and finally eucharistic communion, as the moment of full participation in the mystery that is being celebrated. It is appropriate that at communion there be sung Psalm 117 with the antiphon *"Pascha nostrum"* or Psalm 33 with the antiphon "Alleluia, alleluia, alleluia" or some other song of Easter exultation.

92. It is fitting that in the communion of the Easter Vigil, full expression be given to the symbolism of the Eucharist, namely, by consuming the Eucharist under the species of both bread and wine. The local ordinaries will consider the appropriateness of such a concession and its ramifications.[101]

3. Some Pastoral Considerations

93. The Easter Vigil liturgy should be celebrated in such a way as to offer to the Christian people the riches of the prayers and rites. It is, therefore, important that authenticity be respected, that the participation of the faithful be promoted, and that the celebration should not take place without servers, readers, and choir exercising their roles.

94. It would be desirable if, on occasion, provision were made for several communities to assemble in one church, wherever their proximity to one

---

[98]Cf. ibid., n. 47.

[99]Cf. ibid., n. 49; RCIA, n. 36.

[100]Cf. *Roman Missal*, "The Easter Vigil," n. 53; Ibid., "Ritual Masses," n. 3, Baptism.

[101]GIRM, nn. 240–242.

another or small numbers mean that a full and festive celebration could not otherwise take place.

The celebration of the Easter Vigil for special groups is not to be encouraged since, above all in this Vigil, the faithful should come together as one and should experience a sense of ecclesial community.

The faithful who are absent from their parish should be urged to participate in the liturgical celebration in the place where they happen to be.

95. In announcements concerning the Easter Vigil, care should be taken not to present it as the concluding period of Holy Saturday, but rather it should be stressed that the Easter Vigil is celebrated "during Easter night," and that it is one single act of worship. Pastors should be advised that in giving catechesis to the people, they should be taught to participate in the Vigil in its entirety.[102]

96. For a better celebration of the Easter Vigil, it is necessary that pastors themselves have an ever deeper knowledge of both texts and rites, so as to give a proper mystagogical catechesis to the people.

B. Easter Day

97. Mass is to be celebrated on Easter Day with great solemnity. It is appropriate that the penitential rite on this day take the form of a sprinkling with water blessed at the Vigil, during which the antiphon *"Vidi aquam"* or some other song of baptismal character should be sung. The entrance steps to the church should also be filled with the same water.

98. The tradition of celebrating baptismal Vespers on Easter Day with the singing of psalms during the procession to the font should be maintained where it is still in force and, as appropriate, restored.[103]

99. The paschal candle has its proper place either by the ambo or by the altar and should be lit at least in all the more solemn liturgical celebrations of the season until Pentecost Sunday, whether at Mass or at Morning and Evening Prayer. After the Easter season, the candle should be kept with honor in the baptistery, so that in the celebration of baptism, the candles of the baptised may be lit from them. In the celebration of funerals the paschal candle should be placed near the coffin to indicate that the death of a Christian is his own passover. The paschal candle should not otherwise be lit nor placed in the sanctuary outside the Easter season.[104]

---

[102]Cf. SC, n. 106.

[103]Cf. GILOTH, n. 213.

[104]Cf. *Roman Missal*, "Pentecost Sunday," final rubric; *The Roman Ritual*, "Rite of Baptism for Children," Christian Initiation, General Introduction, n. 25.

VIII. Easter Time

100. The celebration of Easter is prolonged throughout the Easter season. The fifty days from Easter Sunday to Pentecost Sunday are celebrated as one feast day, the "great Sunday."[105]

101. The Sundays of this season are regarded as Sundays of Easter and are so termed; they have precedence over all feasts of the Lord and over all solemnities. Solemnities that fall on one of these Sundays are anticipated on the Saturday.[106] Celebrations in honor of the Blessed Virgin Mary or the saints that fall during the week may not be transferred to one of these Sundays.[107]

102. For adults who have received Christian initiation during the Easter Vigil, the whole of this period is given over to mystagogical catechesis. Therefore, wherever there are neophytes, the prescriptions of the *Ordo initiationis Christianae adultorum*, nn. 37–40 and 235–239, should be observed. Intercession should be made in the Eucharistic Prayer for the newly baptized through the Easter octave in all places.

103. Throughout the Easter season, the neophytes should be assigned their own special place among the faithful. All neophytes should endeavor to participate at Mass along with their godparents. In the homily and, according to local circumstances, in the General Intercessions, mention should be made of them. Some celebration should be held to conclude the period of mystagogical catechesis on or about Pentecost Sunday, depending upon local custom.[108] It is also appropriate that children receive their first communion on one or other of the Sundays of Easter.

104. During Easter time, pastors should instruct the faithful who have been already initiated into the Eucharist on the meaning of the Church's precept concerning the reception of Holy Communion during this period.[109] It is highly recommended that communion also be brought to the sick, especially during the Easter octave.

---

[105]Cf. GNLYC, n. 22.
[106]Cf. ibid., nn. 5, 23.
[107]Cf. ibid., n. 58.
[108]RCIA, nn. 235–239.
[109]CIC, c. 920.

105. Where there is the custom of blessing houses in celebration of the resurrection, this blessing is to be imparted after the Solemnity of Easter and not before, by the parish priest or other priests or deacons delegated by him. This is an opportunity for exercising a pastoral ministry.[110] The parish priest should go to each house for the purpose of undertaking a pastoral visitation of each family. There, he will speak with the residents and spend a few moments with them in prayer, using texts to be found in the book *De Benedictionibus*.[111] In larger cities, consideration should be given to the gathering of several families for a common celebration of the blessing for all.

106. According to the differing circumstances of places and peoples, there are found a number of popular practices linked to celebrations of the Easter season, which in some instances attract greater numbers of the people than the sacred liturgy itself. These practices are not in any way to be undervalued, for they are often well adapted to the religious mentality of the faithful. Let episcopal conferences and local ordinaries, therefore, see to it that practices of this kind, which seem to nourish popular piety, be harmonized in the best way possible with the sacred liturgy, be imbued more distinctly with the spirit of the liturgy, be in some way derived from it, and lead the people to it.[112]

107. This sacred period of fifty days concludes with Pentecost Sunday, when the gift of the Holy Spirit to the apostles, the beginnings of the Church, and the start of its mission to all tongues and peoples and nations are commemorated.[113]

Encouragement should be given to the prolonged celebration of Mass in the form of a Vigil, whose character is not baptismal as in the Easter Vigil, but is one of urgent prayer, after the example of the apostles and disciples, who persevered together in prayer with Mary, the Mother of Jesus, as they awaited the Holy Spirit.[114]

---

[110]Cf. *Maxima redemptionis nostrae mysteria*, n. 24, AAS 47 (1955): 847.

[111]*De Benedictionibus*, caput I, II, Ordo benedictionis annuae familiarium in propriis domibus.

[112]SC, n. 13; Cf. Confraternity of Christian Doctrine, *Orientamentie proposte per la celebrazione dell'anno mariano* (April 3, 1987), nn. 3, 51–56.

[113]Cf. GNLYC, n. 23.

[114]It is possible to combine the celebration of first Vespers with the celebration of Mass as provided for in the *General Instruction of the Liturgy of the Hours*, n. 96. In order to throw into greater relief the mystery of this day, it is possible to have several readings from Holy Scripture, as proposed in the *Lectionary*. In this case, after the collect, the reader goes to the ambo to proclaim the reading. The psalmist or cantor sings the psalm, to which the people respond with the refrain. Then, all stand and the priest says, "Let us pray"; after a short pause, he says the prayer corresponding to the reading (e.g., one of the collects for the ferial days of the Seventh Week of Easter).

108. "It is proper to the paschal festivity that the whole Church rejoices at the forgiveness of sins, which is not only for those who are reborn in Holy Baptism, but also for those who have long been numbered among the adopted children."[115] By means of a more intensive pastoral care and a deeper spiritual effort, all who celebrate the Easter feasts will, by the Lord's grace, experience their effect in their daily lives.[116]

Given at Rome, January 16, 1988.

Paul Augustin Cardinal Mayer
Prefect

+ Virgilio Noè
Titular Archbishop of Voncaria
Secretary

---

[115]St. LEO THE GREAT, *Sermo 6 de Quadragesima*, 1–2, PL 54: 285.

[116]Cf. *Roman Missal*, "Saturday of the Seventh Week of Easter," Opening Prayer.